UNITED STATES OF VIBRAM

International partnership strategy

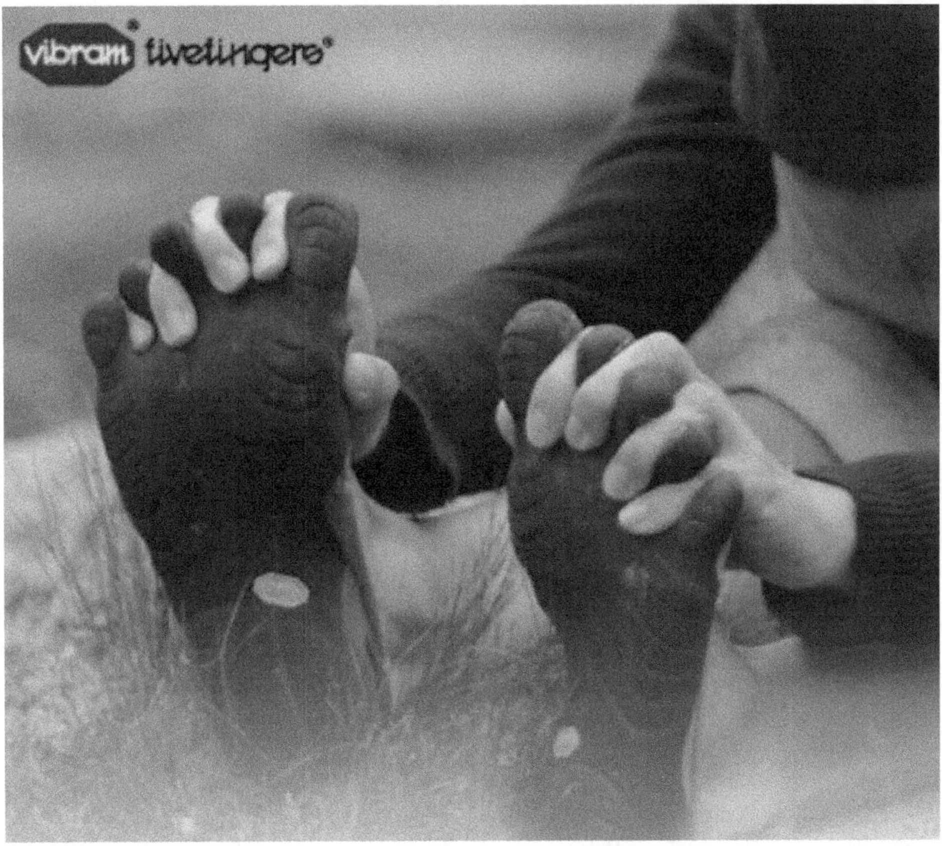

Author:
Mauro Tommaso De Candia

INDEX

Section 1: Introduction to Vibram

Section 2: Partnership in the USA

Section 3: SWOT analysis of Vibram

Section 4: Business Portfolio Analysis

Section 5: Market segmentation and competitive position

Section 6: Double Screening process for new countries

Section 7: Market entry strategy for Vibram Five Fingers

Appendix 1: Evolution of the indices

Appendix 2: Graphic illustration of the balance sheet

Appendix 3: Graphic illustration of the company's profits

Bibliography

SECTION 1: INTRODUCTION TO VIBRAM

Vibram is an Italian company set in Albizzate, in the province of Varese, that produces rubber soles for shoes, especially shoes intended for use in the mountains' climbing. The company is named after its founder, Vitale Bramani.

Bramani is credited with inventing the first rubber lug soles for shoes. These soles were first used on mountaineering boots, replacing leather soles fitted with hobnails or steel cleats, commonly used up until then.

In 1935, the deaths of six of Bramani's mountaineering friends in the Italian Alps were partly blamed on inadequate footwear. The tragedy drove Bramani to develop a new climbing sole.

Two years later, he patented his invention and launched the first rubber lug soles on the market with a tread design called the "Carrarmato", with the financial backing of Leopoldo Pirelli of Pirelli tires. The sole was designed to provide excellent traction on the widest range of surfaces, have a high degree of abrasion resistance and was made using the latest vulcanized rubber of the time. In 1954, the first successful ascent to the summit of K2 was made by an Italian expedition wearing Vibram rubber on their soles.

Today, Vibram concentrate in Italy, which remains the heart of the company, strategic business activities such as industrial design, managerial and strategic functions, new technology and new product development. This is done to guarantee all clients Vibram quality, wherever they are. Thanks to this organizational structure, Vibram has remained the world leader in rubber soling.

Commercial and production facilities are located close to the markets that the company is present in, namely United States, Brazil, Japan and China.

Vibram's partner in the United States is Quabaug Corporation, who has been a licensed manufacturer of Vibram for over 40 years. Located in North Brookfield, MA, the company specializes in the working, military, hunting and safety markets of North America. 2009 saw the start-up of the futuristic Vibram Technological Center in Huadu (Guang Dong region) China.

Vibram is well known for pioneering the barefoot running movement with the FiveFingers line of shoes that mimic the look and mechanics of being barefoot, consisting of foot gloves to facilitate natural foot movement and traction while engaging in sporting activities. The new type of shoe FiveFingers was named by Time magazine one of the best inventions of 2007.

Although the brand is best known among the outdoor and mountaineering community, Vibram produces numerous models of soles specifically designed for fashion, military, rescue, law enforcement, bicycling, motorcycling, water and snow sports or industrial use. Vibram also produces soles used exclusively for footwear resoling.

These are some brands that make use of Vibram soles in their footwear offerings: Merrel, Timberland, Nike ACG, Lowa, Scarpa, Asolo, La Sportiva, Vasque, Montrail New Balance, Rockport, and Florshim.

Although the first models of soles were made of vulcanized natural rubber, currently employ synthetic compounds, which may be composed of about 15-20 different ingredients (including for example, sulfur, carbon, silicon) which profoundly affect the performance of the finished product.

Capital share

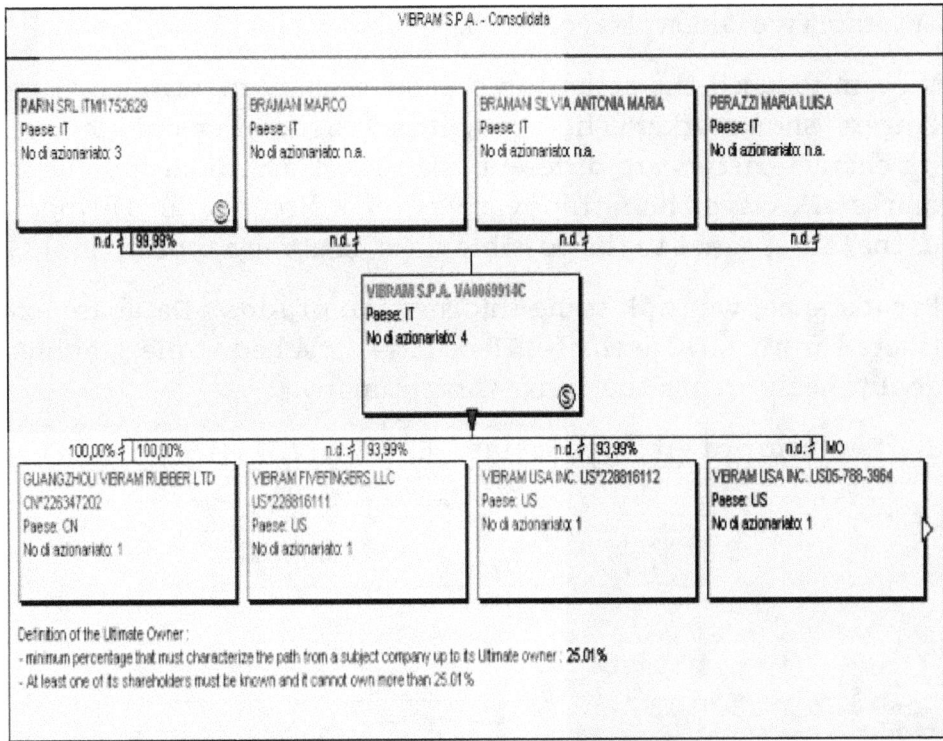

Vibram is a SME leader in its sector basically because of its products: shoes with a special sole that enhance the ability to engage in extreme sports (mainly climbing and mountaineering), while its Vibram five fingers product line help the users' feet adapt better to the different pavements using the natural physiology of the human foot.

Vibram is ranked at the top in the world in this type of shoes, mainly because it gained a long experience and a unique "Know-How". The company has become the undisputed leader of technologically advanced soles for a wide range of shoes offering high performances, maximum level of comfort and quality that are able to endure the test of time. This level of comfort is granted by the rigorous tests that are carried out in laboratory and on its own "Vibram Tester Team ground".

Vibram is an example of the constant commitment in research and development of innovative solutions through the creation of

"Vibram Five Fingers" revolution.

Vibram focused the attention on this already mentioned "Five Fingers" shoe market. This product is designed in a unique way; its characteristics are different than the traditional foot wear market. However, being innovative in this direction also bring to us the "acceptance to the possible risks" that may appear.

For instance, we took some information of Aida's Database extracted from LIUC website. Here it is attached some graphics about the internal situation of this company:

2.1. Evolution of Vibram's Society- EBITDA (2011)

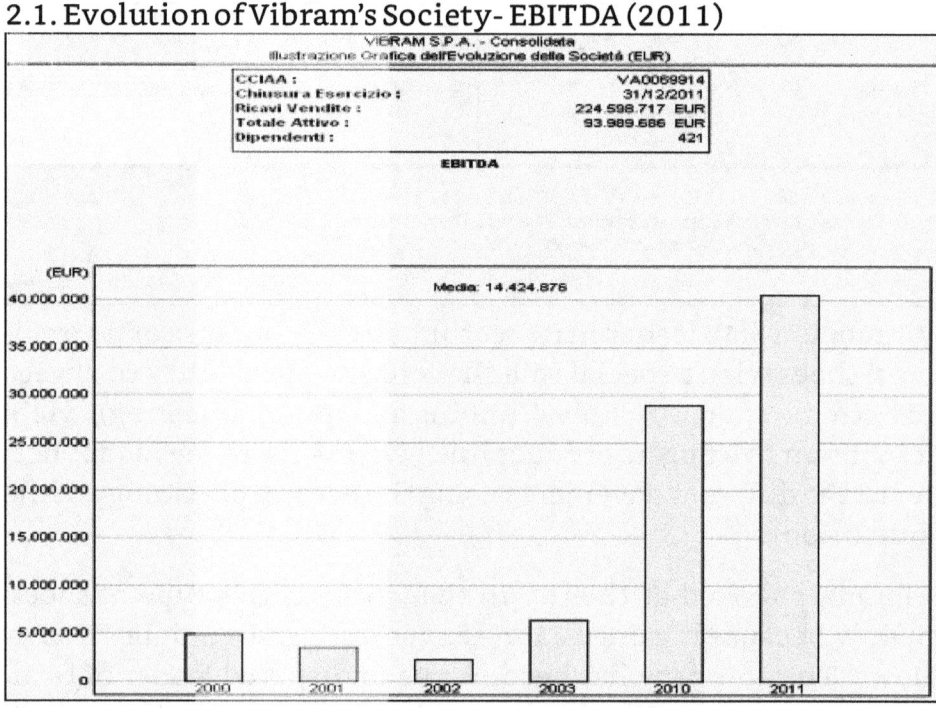

As we can see in the evolution of Vibram's society, figure 2.1, in 2000 the net profit it's around 5 million € while in 2001 and 2002 we can see that descends almost by the half of the amount obtained in 2000. However, in 2003, 2010 and finally 2011 this company increment their EBITDA until reach a surprising amount of 40 million €.

2.2. Evolution EBITDA/SELLING (2011)

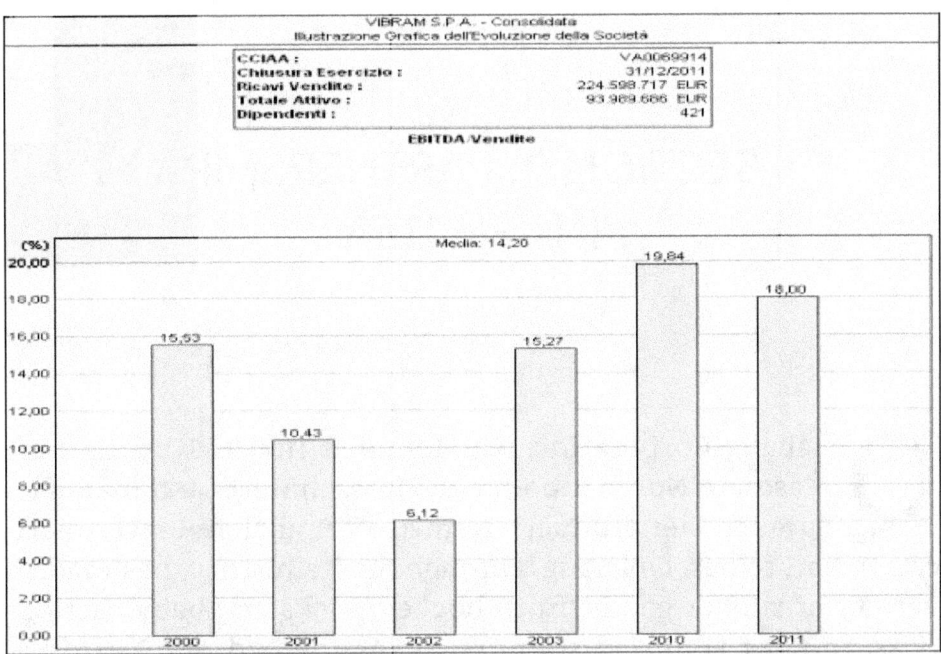

As we can see on the figure 2.2, about the evolution EBITDA/SELLING, in 2000 it represents 15,53% while as commented previously on figure 2.1 in 2001 and 2003 it decrements to 10,43% and 6.12%. Moreover, there is a strong increment of Earnings before interest, taxes, depreciations and amortizations divided by selling from 2003 till 2011, going from 15,27% to finally reach 18%. In addition, there is a fact that has to be mentioned, there is a short decrease from 2010 to 2011 approximately by a 2%. As a result we can conclude that 2010 have the higher percentage corresponding to 19,84%.

SECTION 2: PARTNERSHIP IN THE USA

Quabaug Corporation was founded in 1916 by Herbert Mason in North Brookfield, Massachusetts and manufactures rubber products. Named after ancient local American Indian tribes, Quabaug, throughout its history, has made a variety of rubber goods: from hockey pucks and baby carriage tires, to floor tiles and stair treads. At the end of 1940, Quabaug started focusing on the production of shoe soles and now it manufactures technologically advanced shoe soles for a variety of uses. The company's history is full of achievements in innovation.

In 1937 were introduced in the market, soles made with a synthetic material called DuPont neoprene. In 1945, Quabaug has received an award from the U.S. Army and Navy for the quality of its military products.

In 1961, they produced the first one-piece sole, which was easier to manufacture and more convenient for the customer. In 1962, Quabaug introduced the Hypalon, a synthetic material that DuPont had a better wear resistance than the standard at the time, making it perfect for use in casual shoes.

In 1965 began the partnership between the legendary Italian shoe sole manufacturer Vibram and Quabaug. Since 1965, Quabaug has been the U.S. exclusive manufacturer and licensee of Vibram soling products. Vibram soles are used in some of the most demanding environments: by firefighters in Arizona or the combat units in the mountains of Afghanistan. Vibram soles are reliable to provide performance when it matters most.

In 1967, they introduced Nitrile rubber, a compound resistant to oils, guaranteed for the duration of the shoe.

After the acquisition of the soles division of the Biltrite Corporation in 2002, Quabaug now has more than 300 employees and is committed to the development of new projects.

Quabaug is proud to be the leading provider of soles for the U.S. military and to be producing in the United States. At the base of Quabaug there is a culture of continuous improvement and unwavering dedication to quality, this is the secret of its success.[1]

SECTION 3: SWOT ANALYSIS OF VIBRAM

The SWOT analysis is a tool of the strategic management and a great device to analyze the current strategy of an enterprise. With this tool we would like to outline again the company's external and internal situation.
Our aim is to combine the firm's analysis with business portfolio analysis to decide which could be in our opinion a possible target countries for the future, having bare in mind that Vibram should still conserve and develop market where is already present.

Strengths
It's important to consider the company's strengths from the internal perspective and also from the customers' point of view.
Vibram has a very important brand history in the market, was founded in the 1937, and consequently has an enormous know how producing soles and is everywhere recognized and appreciated for its soles materials and characteristics.
The firm has patents for protecting its brands (Vibram and Five Fingers) and these represent a form of protection, or a kind of defensive barrier against its competitors and counterfeit products.
It is highly renowned for its ability to offer technologically advanced and high quality soles, and so a sort of sure investment for customers and so those characteristics lead to brand awareness: is the extent to which the consumer associates the brand with the product he desires to buy.
The firm founded by Vittorio Bramani has commercial and productive structures in the world: USA, China, Japan and Brazil; so it

could easily react to changes in those foreign markets and economize on costs of production and costs of sending its products all around the world.

Vibram in the 1965 signed an important partnership with Quabaug, a renowned and well recognized firm, that is structured for develop design and activities.

Quabaug has important cooperation with most famous North American brands: Red Wing, Wolverine, Belleville, Denner, and HH Brown.

A strength of Vibram is that it not only has its own local authorized retailers, but also distributes his products on the web: in fact, it has an own online shop (for the B2C market: Five Fingers authorized shop) and many authorized shops either for Vibram's sponsored shoes or for Five Fingers.

Furthermore, it has a strong the brand image, which is equally important: Vibram is synonymous worldwide for well-manufactured, resistant and durable products, perfect either for new costumers or for existing customers, with keen knowledge about technical shoes.

Vibram supplies its outsoles to all the most important producers of mountain shoes (Asolo, The North Face, and Timberland, just to quote some brands) Their name recognition and their good image on the European and international market are also an excellent base for future marketing strategies and tactics.

Weaknesses

And again, it's necessary to consider the weaknesses from an internal and external point of view. Customers could see weaknesses that the company can't see, for example as a Vibram also tries to serve just a strict segment (niche) of consumers and this leads to a very narrow potential target group. The threat can be the loss of their actual and sole target group.

Is possible also that Vibram has high costs of because the fact that all research and development is confined in the centre of Albizzate.

Another weakness is that spreading out the production all

around the world, by one side it save costs of transport, by the other side doesn't realize economies of scale.

Considering the external way of looking at this business, we have to criticize the price of Vibram products. It's easy to find shoes with similar features, for a price less than what you would have to pay for a pair of shoes with a sole branded Vibram. For instance Decathlon offers many shoes with a lower price. Nevertheless the price can also been seen as an indicator for high quality and special technical characteristics, especially the customers are often following these pattern of thinking.

Opportunities

Opportunities are the result of using the company's strength to get the advantage of their competitors. Alternatively opportunities could come along by eliminating their own weaknesses. Vibram got into a well-established position on the European and international market with a well-defined market niche.

The company's opportunity is to use their strength and try to expand their market position. Regarding the weaknesses which should be eliminated it's worth to mention their narrow target group. Furthermore, Vibram has the possibility to expand its market targeting new growing country (Brazil, India and again China), continuing the process of expansion started in the 2009 with the Vibram China Technological Center and the flagship store in Boston in the 2012.

Vibram could also implement sponsorships and to build marketing campaigns to confirm position either on B2C or on B2B market.

We think that sponsorships should be done using Five Fingers shoes, because the logo on those is easily to be seen by the customer and easily recognizable.

We think about something like celebrity endorsement, for increasing brand recognition of our firm.

We think also that Vibram could project other shoes with its brand, like Fivefingers, to consolidate the position on the B2C market.

Threats

Like opportunities do, threats have their origin in external effects. The characteristics of threats are their propensity to cause trouble concerning the operational effectiveness and the company's economic viability. The company's threats should be eliminated by using their strengths. According to this, also the other way round, the threats should be eliminated by reducing their weaknesses. As mentioned just before headed by "weaknesses" the threat consists of the loss of their sole target group during periods of economic instability and periods of economic decrease. In such periods people give up buying technical high quality and higher price shoes and soles like Vibram products. People limit their consumption to the bare necessities, like food. In case of doubt they will buy cheaper shoes (and consequently cheaper soles), disregarding the quality and technicality. Another omnipresent threat is the danger of counterfeit products, for instance from the Far Eastern regions, such as China. Counterfeit soles could seem to be Vibram and actually they are poor-quality and with a low resistance. Clients could be cheated by these products. It's also possible that this pirated material causes a bad reputation. To counteract this phenomenon, Vibram should concentrate on informing their customers about their quality characteristics and continuing to do specific patents against counterfeit, like is already doing.

SECTION 4: BUSINESS PORTFOLIO ANALYSIS

To analyse current markets of Vibram we decide to use two different, matrices that we analysed in depth during our course: Boston Consulting Group and the Key Country Matrix.

The aim of these matrices is the same one: the analysis of current portfolio, either for business or for countries.

In our case we want to focus of countries analysis to understand where should Vibram invest and which countries should be retained.

First we use the Boston Consulting group to analyse Vibram's portfolio because is possible to say that is a simplified version of the Key Country Matrix having less variables, in the BCG we have <u>Economic Growth</u> instead of <u>Market Attractiveness</u> (has a broader range of factors), <u>Market Share</u> is a substitute of <u>Competitive Strength</u> and being finally a 2*2 matrix instead than a 3*3.

We decide to choose two developed countries and two developing countries, also to analyse which category of country offer the best opportunities for a future market entry strategy that is the final aim of our project.

Like developing countries we choose the most representative in the portfolio of Vibram two market share and potential growth and also for the country future development that are: China and Brazil.

When are asked to decide about the two developed countries our first thoughts were Europe, for the presence pf the country in which our firm was created and developed, and North America, for the presence of an historical partnership with Quabaug, fundamental for the development of the firm, especially for the American market.

Analysing countries we found that the most attractive in terms of market share and market growth is China: especially for the increasing number of rich young rich people that could be particularly interested in the purchase of a sophisticated and high performant product like Vibram.

Another feature that was important in our decision is the presence on the Chinese ground of an important research centre called 'Vibram China Tech Center' with the aim of: increasing Vibram's technologies and to build relationships with the most important Chinese retailers and distributors.

Using the nickname given by the inventor of the Matrix is possible to say that Europe and USA are 'Cash Cows': they are the oldest market (Europe is still older than USA) and they are the centrepiece, which has to support the growth of Vibram in the emerging market.

Not only Europe but also in the North America the presence of Vibram is strong: also speaking about North America Vibram placed in the 2001 the US Commercial Headquarters near Boston, in Concord Massachusetts with the final aim of increasing again brand awareness and penetration of the market.

We already spoke about the importance of the partnership with Quabaug.

We decide to put a question mark on Brazil because in our opinion Vibram should invest further on this market because at the moment the firm shouldn't be consider it an important source for the future.

In our personal opinion Brazil is one of the top interesting market, probably the only one in the South America that could be a perspective for the future: also for the opportunity of growth.

Another lack of the firm in this country is the non-presence of commercial or research structures.

This is a representation of the previously utilized matrix, useful to have a general look at the country portfolio analysis.

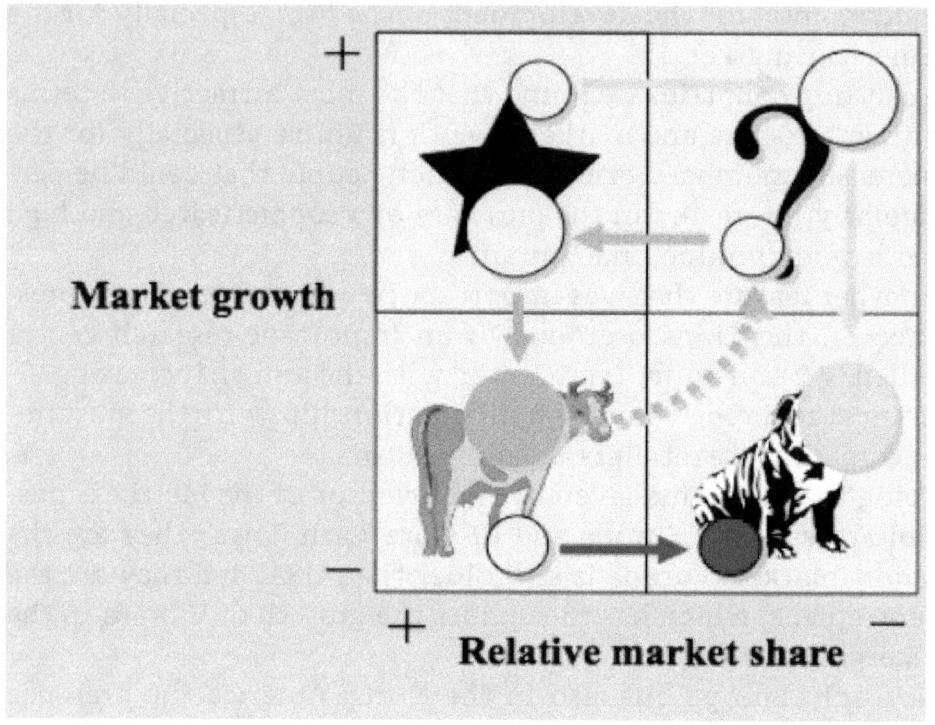

SECTION 5: MARKET SEGMENTATION AND COMPETITIVE POSITION

This section will analyse the global footwear market using Porter's Five Forces as an analytical tool. Considering Vibram's international presence, it will be appropriate to analyse the footwear industry in a global context. This will help to highlight some of the market challenges as well as provide insight into some of the emerging trends in the market. It is also important to note that Vibram is both an outsole manufacturer (B2B) and a retailer (B2C), thus playing a dual role of a market player as well as supplier to the footwear market. This will also be taken into consideration in our analysis.

Market definition:

- The footwear market consists of the total revenues generated through the sale of all types of men, women and children shoes.
- For the purposes of this report, the global market consists of North America, South America, Western Europe, Eastern Europe, MEA, and Asia-Pacific.
    - **North America** consists of Canada, Mexico, and the United States.
    - **South America** comprises Argentina, Brazil, Chile, Colombia, and Venezuela.

- **Western Europe** comprises Belgium, Denmark, France, Germany, Greece, Italy, the Netherlands, Norway, Spain, Sweden, Switzerland, Turkey, and the United Kingdom.
- **Eastern Europe** comprises the Czech Republic, Hungary, Poland, Romania, Russia, and Ukraine.
- **Asia-Pacific** comprises Australia, China, India, Indonesia, Japan, New Zealand, Singapore, South Korea, Taiwan, and Thailand.
- **Middle East-Africa (MEA)** comprises Egypt, Israel, Nigeria, Saudi Arabia, South Africa, and United Arab Emirates.

Market Analysis[2]:

The global footwear market has grown moderately in recent years. Accelerated growth is expected for the forecast period through to 2017. The global footwear market had total revenues of €184.6bn in 2012, representing a compound annual growth rate (CAGR) of 3.5% between 2008 and 2012. In comparison, the European and Asia-Pacific markets grew with CAGRs of 1.7% and 4.8% respectively, over the same period, to reach respective values of €70.8bn and €35.2bn in 2012.

Clothing, footwear, sportswear and accessories retailers accounted for the largest proportion of sales in the global footwear market in 2012; sales through this channel generated €124.3bn, equivalent to 67.4% of the market's overall value. Sales through department stores generated revenues of €29.4bn in 2012, equating to 15.9% of the market's aggregate revenues.

The performance of the market is forecasted to accelerate, with an anticipated CAGR of 4.9% for the five -year period 2012 - 2017, that is expected to drive the market to a value of €234.9bn by the end of 2017. Comparatively, the European and Asia-Pacific markets will grow with CAGRs of 2.5% and 5.9% respectively, over the same period, to reach respective values of €80.1bn and €46.8bn in 2017.

Market Value:

The global footwear market grew by 3.7% in 2012 to reach a value of €184.5 billion. The compound annual growth rate of the market in the period 2008–12 was 3.5%.

Table 1: Global footwear market value: € billion, 2008-12			
Year	$ Billion	€ Billion	% Growth YOY
2008	223.80	160.80	
2009	227.00	163.20	1.5%
2010	237.50	170.70	4.6%
2011	247.40	177.80	4.2%
2012	256.60	184.50	3.8%
CAGR 2008 - 12			3.5%

Source: Market Line

Figure 1: Global footwear market value: € billion, 2008-12

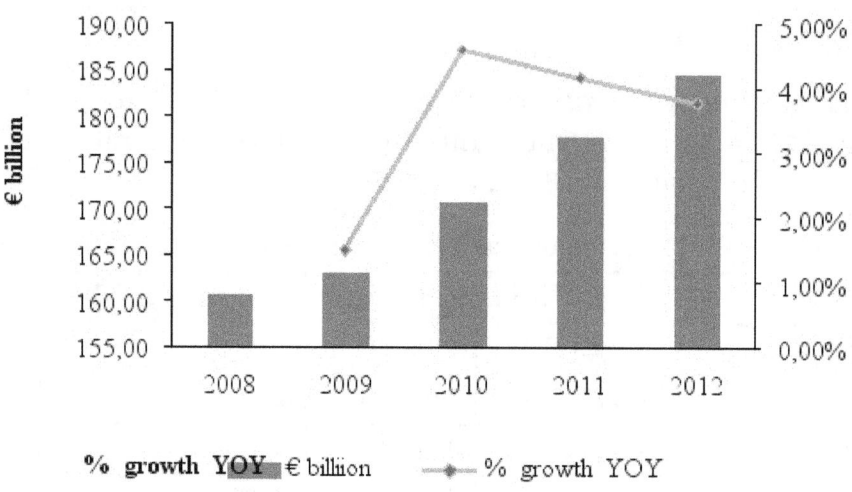

Source: Market Line

Market segmentation:

The Americas account for 38.4% of the global footwear market value, while
Europe accounts for a further 38.4% of the global market.

Table 2: Global footwear market geography segmentation: € billion, 2012		
Geography	2012	%
Americas	70.9	38.4
Europe	70.8	38.4
Asia-Pacific	35.3	19.1
Middle East & Africa	7.5	4.1
Total	169.5	100

Source: Market Line

Figure 2: Global footwear market geography segmentation: $ billion, 2012

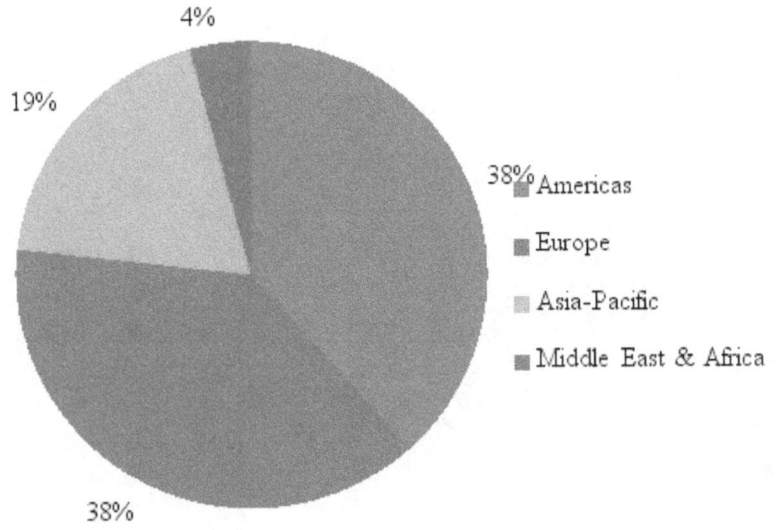

- 38% Americas
- 38% Europe
- 19% Asia-Pacific
- 4% Middle East & Africa

Source: Market Line

Market distribution:

Clothing/footwear/sportswear/accessories retailers form the leading distribution channel in the global footwear market, accounting for a 67.4% share of the total market's value. Department stores account for a further 15.9% of the market.

Table 3: Global footwear market distribution: % share, by value, 2012	
Channel	% Share
Clothing/footwear/sportswear/accessories retailers	67.4
Department stores	15.9
Hypermarket, supermarket, & discounters	8.1
Other	8.6

| Total | 100 |

Source: Market Line

Figure 3: Global footwear market distribution: % share, by value, 2012

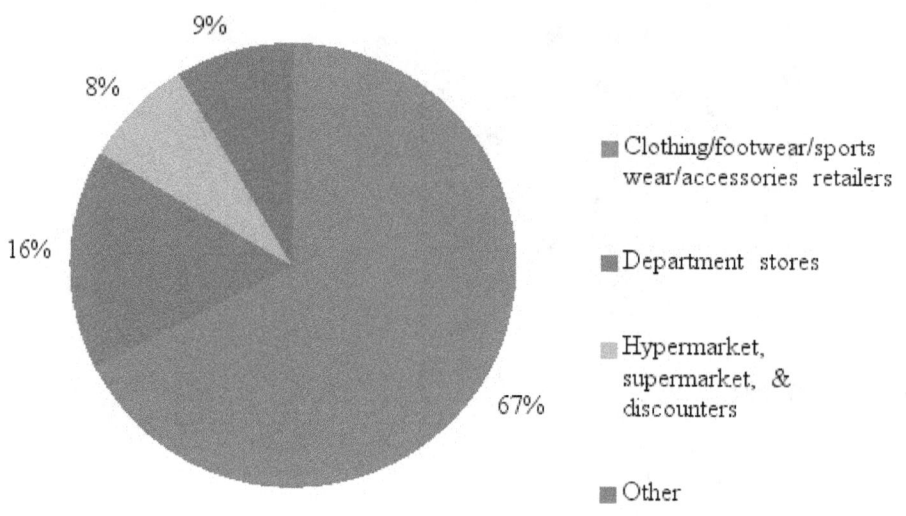

Source: Market Line

Market Value forecast:

In 2017, the global footwear market is forecast to have a value of €234.7 billion, an increase of 27.2% since 2012. The compound annual growth rate of the market in the period 2012–17 is predicted to be 4.9%.

Table 4: Global footwear market value forecast, € billion, 2012-17			
Year	$ Billion	€ Billion	% Growth YOY
2012	256.6	184.5	3.7%
2013	268	192.6	4.4%
2014	280.4	201.6	4.6%

2015	294.2	211.5	4.9%
2016	309.6	222.5	5.2%
2017	326.5	234.7	5.5%

Source: Market Line

Figure 4: Global footwear market value forecast, € billion, 2012-17

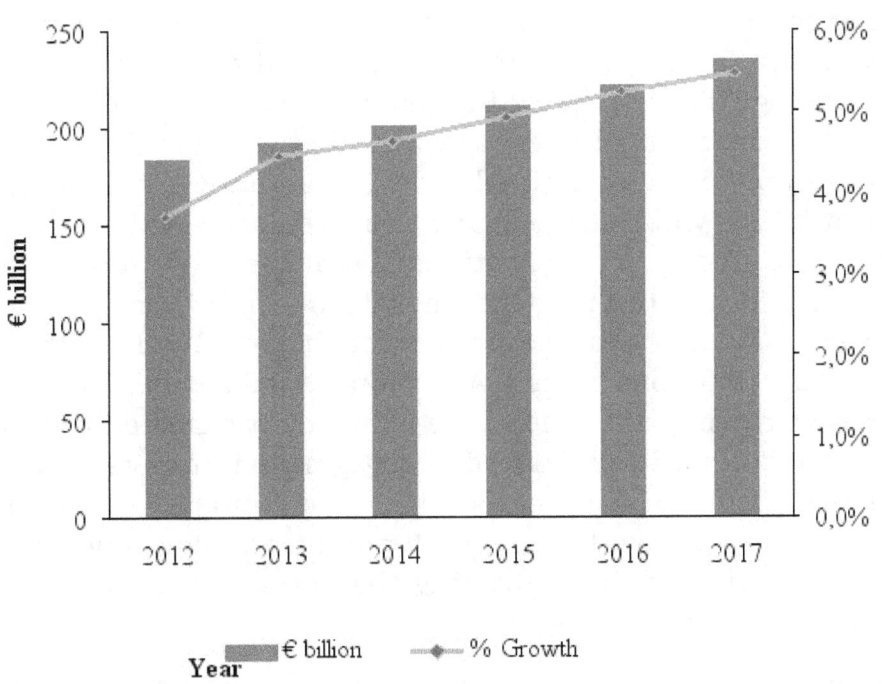

Source: Market Line

Vibram's competitive position

Now that we have gained a better understanding of the footwear market, we can proceed to appraise Vibram's competitive position. Vibram is well positioned to compete internationally with representative offices in four out of six geographical areas defined in this report. In particular, Vibram has offices in North-America (USA), South America (Brazil), Europe (Headquarters in Italy) and Asia-Pacific (Japan and China). The opening of the Technological Centre in China in 2009 is the most recent effort in strengthening its presence international market and increase synergy with the geographical market it serves.

Buyer Power: Vibram recognizes that it serves a niche market and thus buyers have high bargaining power due to the need for shoes and outsoles that ensure safety, performance and functionality.

Supplier Power: As a supplier, Vibram possesses higher supplier power compared to its peers because of its ability to differentiate its offerings through the design and manufacture of an array of outsoles targeted at different sport, industrial and military uses. For example, its VSM technology soles are built for sliding in motor biking while also offering sole interchangeability, while its soles for industrial applications have anti-electric shock capabilities etc. Its latest product innovation – the Vibram Five Fingers is yet another effort to differentiate its brand and products, and a successful one indeed. As a pioneer and advocate for the barefoot running movement, the company has created to new niche market for itself, instead of engaging in intensive competition in saturated footwear markets. The Vibram Five Fingers serves more as a glove than a shoe. It provides the consumer with feet protection while facilitating the natural movement and flexibility of the human foot.

Vibram has been able build brand equity by providing quality products that have been tested for safety by its own Vibram Tester Team in collaboration with real athletes. Furthermore, Vibram has successfully built up a reputation, as a company that has the right expertise and experience to understand customer needs with respect to the sports that they play as well as the hazardous jobs that they do. As an alpine mountaineer himself, the owner brings credibility to the brand and company vision.

New entrants: In the perspective of Vibram, we think that the threat of new entrants is not as strong as the overall market. Vibram has been active in protecting its technology and designs with patents while being quick to innovate, beating imitators to the market. Furthermore, Vibram recognize the need to be close to its market and its suppliers, having offices in the United States, Brazil, Japan and China. With the establishment of its Hangzhou Technological Innovation Centre as it's most active involvement in Asia yet.

Threat of substitutes: The threat of substitution of Vibram products is weak, which remains in line with the overall market assessment. This is because Vibram operates in a niche market segment where they produce specialty soles for specific uses that are not substituted by shoes and soles from other market segments. Despite the existence of knock-offs and counterfeit products, it is reasonable to assume both B2C and B2B customers/clients remain vigilant in the selection of authentic Vibram shoes and outsoles, that suits the dangerous and hazardous environment that require shoes and outsoles made for specialty applications.

Degree of rivalry: This dimension shall be discussed in light of the fact that Vibram competes in a niche market. At the moment, there are not many producers of specialty outsoles in the market, and Vibram has established itself as a company with a long history and over time while developing notable technical expertise to provide consumers with the high level of product performance required to deal with the sole damage come with the extreme sports and industrial/military vocation (while at the same time protecting the users foot). This high brand value already puts Vibram ahead of the minimal competition that exists. Furthermore, Vibram distributes its products through authorized retailers, its own online store as well as through authorized retailers. The firm is still able to maintain high control over the sale of the products and is able to reduce the degree of rivalry between the different distribution channels by selling a different range of products through different sales channels. Being an outsole manufacturer and a market player, this dual role allows the firm to enjoy high synergy through a nuanced form of forward integration between the two value chain functions, allowing it to understand and hence serve the market more effectively. Potential benefits include higher service levels and better market timing for new product entry. All in all, the degree of rivalry in Vibram's niche market segment is considered weak.

Future Trends

A look at the macroeconomic data provides signals about the market trend. Growth data from *Market Line* databases suggests that the Chinese and Asia Pacific market should be the firm's next point of focus (in terms of geographic area), as these markets exhibit higher growth relative to the broad market. Furthermore, China and Asia Pacific markets are expected to further diverge from the global growth, indicating high potential in terms of revenue growth for Vibram.

Figure 5: Comparative market value forecast: % Growth YOY, 2012-17

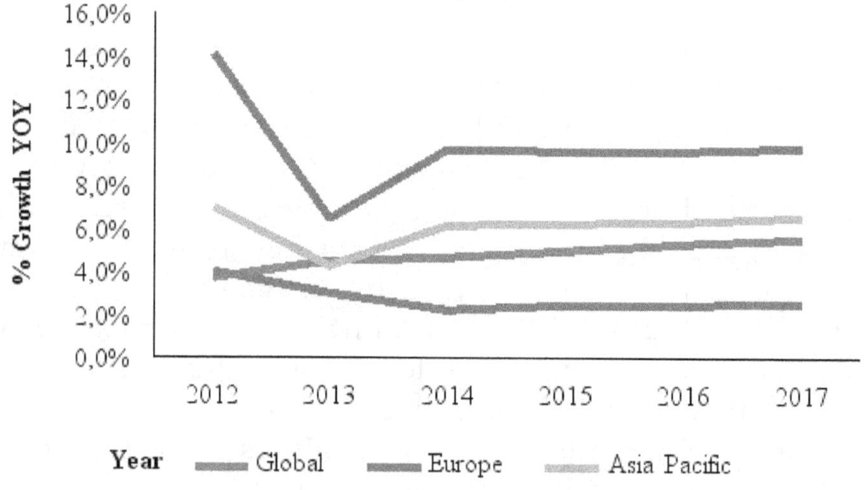

Source: Market Line

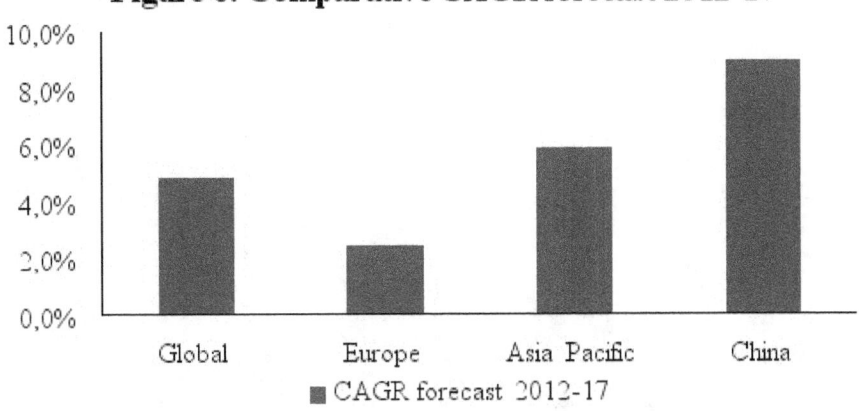

Figure 6: Comparative CAGR forecast 2012-17

Source: Market Line

In light of Vibram's opening of the innovation sector in China, we can see that the firm is already riding on this trend. We see this as a prudent strategic move by the firm, that is likely to pay dividends in the form of revenue growth in the years to come as the Chinese market remains one that is filled with potential.

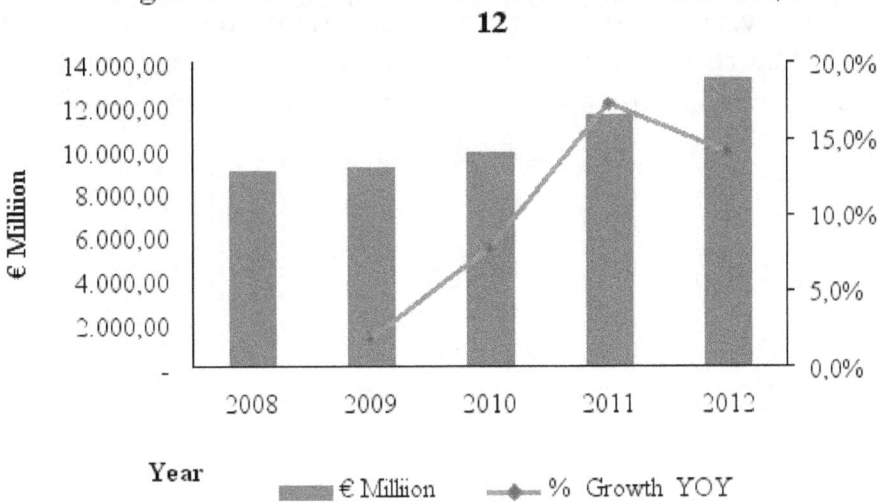

Figure 7: China footwear market value: € million, 2008–12

Source: Market Line

Figure 8: China footwear market value forecast: € million, 2012-17

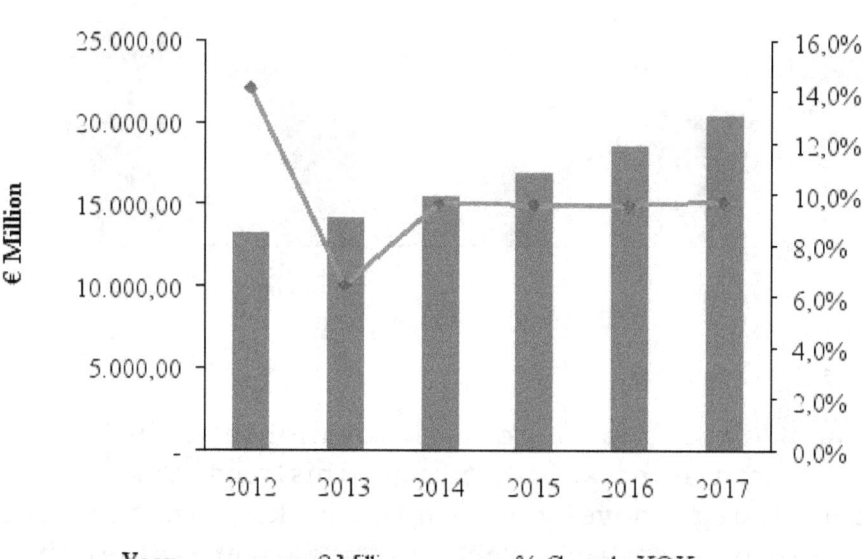

Source: Market Line

Additionally, considering a growing Asian middle class, expenditure in health and wellness is expected to increase, and this bodes well for Vibram as the size of its niche market is expected to grow with this trend.

Figure 9: Asia-Pacific footwear market value: € billion, 2008–12

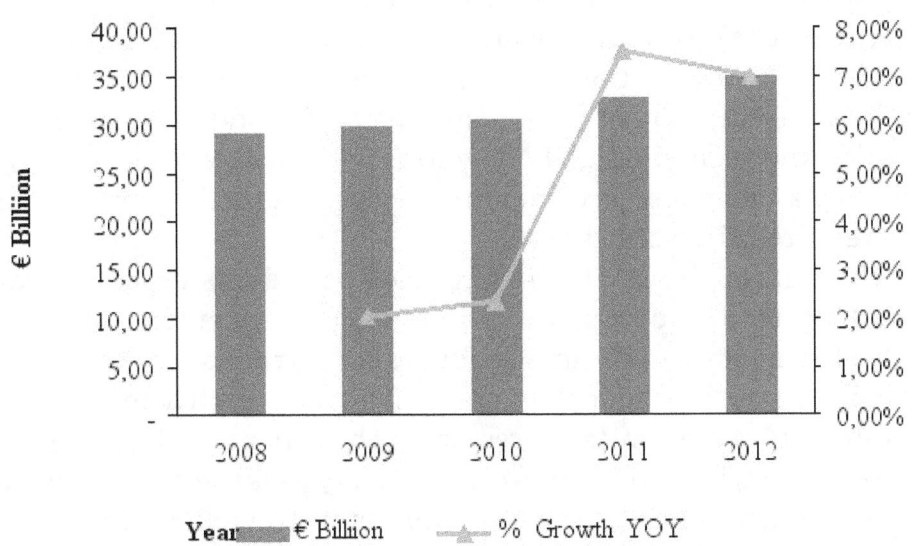

Source: Market Line

Again, we utilize a business portfolio analysis matrix to understand which the main markets of Vibram are. It is important to explain which are the variables that we choose for this matrix, respectively for **Market Attractiveness** and **Competitive Position**.
About **Market Attractiveness,** we decided to analyse weather, population, income per capita and market size.
About **Competitive attractiveness** (business strength), we chose to utilize number of competitors, brand awareness, market share and cost of investments.
The second step was to define weight that has to be attached to drivers: we decide, for market attractiveness, to attach the higher weight to population, then income per capita, followed by market size and weather (we thought about Five Fingers especially, that because are for running, barefoot running, could be a problem to marketize it in a country with a particular climate, e.g.: Russia)
Speaking about competitive positioning we attached the higher weight to number of competitors (important in an almost niche

like the sector of Vibram: presence of already established and renowned competitors can be harmful for the Italian firm), then we have market share, brand awareness and cost of investments.

We decide to attach the lower weight to cost of investments because we retain not so important costs of productions in a top quality and technologically developed sector like soles: nobody will buy a cheaper sole, either for running or for climbing if it has not required characteristics.

On the market is possible to find copycap products, especially for Five Fingers, but looking at reviews is very difficult to say that they are threats for Vibram's products and so this is why we prefer to concentrate on other characteristics of competitiveness.

Result of KCM are similar to results of the other matrix, but with an exception, indeed Brazil from our analysis is the country with the highest potential, especially for its strategic position (Mercosur is a reality that is becoming bigger and bigger) and for the characteristics of growth and development of the country.

Compared with the other matrix we find China lowered for problems especially about climate, in some regions rigid and for a brand awareness still lower that EU and USA.

We are that China also thanks to the strategic building location of a commercial office in Tokyo to promote further Vibram's image and to spread knowledge of the brand on the Chinese ground.

Business Portfolio Analysis let us thinking that developing countries, like Brazil and China should be correctly supported by developed countries to increase Vibram's market share and brand awareness, thanks to favourable conditions: increasing population, increasing GDP per capita, for instance and also that is going to increase further customers that seek sophisticated and top quality products and absolutely reliable, that are the main characteristics of Vibram soles and barefoot running shoes.

○	EUROPE	○	CHINA
○	USA	●	BRAZIL

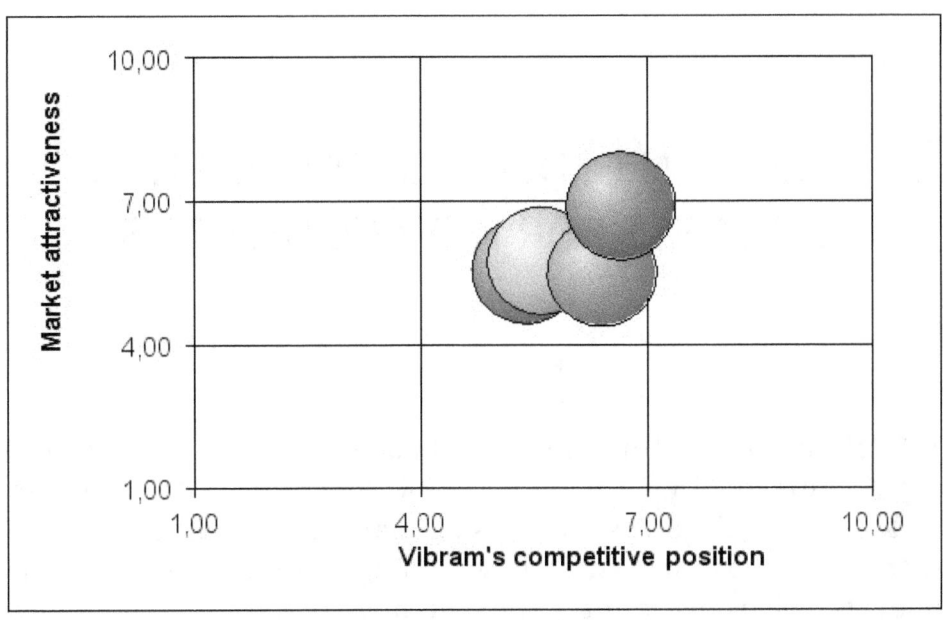

SECTION 6: DOUBLE SCREENING PROCESS FOR NEW COUNTRIES

Vibram is selling his special shoes "Vibram Five Fingers" already in a lot of different countries. They licensed authorized distributors in many countries around the world. The goal of this double screening process is to determine one attractive new country and to define a market entry strategy.

Vibram is at the moment selling directly to customers and retailers in most European countries, USA, Canada, Mexico, China, Hong Kong, Macau and Mongolia.

In other countries "Vibram Five Fingers" are imported and sold by authorized distributors: in Argentina, Australia, Botswana, Brazil, Chile, Colombia, Iceland, India, Israel, Japan, Jordan, Korea, Kuwait, Kazakhstan, Lebanon, Malaysia, Namibia, New Zealand, Oman, Philippines, Puerto Rico, Qatar, Russia, Saudi Arabia, Singapore, South Africa, South Korea, Taiwan, Turkey, United Arab Emirates, Uruguay

To find attractive countries to enter, we chose to take a look at the top emerging markets:

Table: The top 30 Emerging Markets for 2012-2017

Rank	Country	% Respondents
1	India	66.4%
2	Brazil	65.7%
3	China	65.4%

4	Russia	39.7%
5	Indonesia	27.4%
6	South Africa	22.2%
7	Vietnam	20.1%
8	Mexico	18.5%
9	Turkey	17.8%
10	Argentina	10.3%
11	Thailand	9.5%
12	Chile	9.3%
13	South Korea	8.6%
14	Malaysia	8.4%
15	Singapore	8.1%
16	Nigeria	7.7%
17	Colombia	7.4%
18	Saudi Arabia	7.4%
19	Poland	7.0%
20	Philippines	6.7%
21	UAE	6.0%
22	Egypt	5.1%
23	Taiwan	4.9%
24	Hong Kong	4.6%
25	Peru	4.6%
26	Romania	4.2%
27	Czech Republic	3.7%
28	Bangladesh	3.0%
29	Pakistan	3.0%
30	Hungary	2.3%

Source: Global Intelligence Alliance's Business Perspectives on Emerging Markets 2012-2017 Report

The only countries from this list, where Vibram isn't selling directly or through partners are Indonesia, Vietnam, Thailand, Nigeria, Egypt, Peru, Bangladesh and Pakistan. These countries are selected for the double screening process.

Initial Screening

In the first screening the macro environment of the countries is analyzed with indicators of market potential.
(Data from CIA World Factbook: https://www.cia.gov/library/publications/the-world-factbook,
The Economist Intelligence Unit: www.eiu.com)

Indonesia

- **Demographic characteristics:**
    - Population size: 251,160,124 (July 2013 est.)
    - Growth rate: 0.99% (2013 est.)
    - Urban population: 50,7% of total population (2011)
- **Economic Factors:**
    - GDP (purchasing power parity): $1.237 trillion (2012 est.)
    - GDP - real growth rate: 6.2% (2012 est.)
    - GDP - per capita (PPP): $5,100 (2012 est.)
- **Geographic characteristics:**
    - Size: 1,904,569 sq. km
    - Climate: tropical; hot, humid; more moderate in highlands
- **Political risk:** The president, Susilo Bambang Yudhoyono, has a strong mandate to govern, but the achievements of his second-term administration have disappointed. Prospects for further economic reforms are slim, given that politicians are now focusing on the par-

liamentary and presidential elections due in 2014.
- **Economic structure risk:** The government's lack of progress on reforming inflexible labor laws will deter investment, as will a rising number of sector regulations. The Anti-Corruption Commission (KPK) is keeping graft in the spotlight.

Vietnam

- **Demographic characteristics**
    - Population size: 92,477,857 (July 2013 est.)
    - Population growth rate: 1.03% (2013 est.)
    - Urban population: 31% of total population (2011)
- **Economic Factors:**
    - GDP (purchasing power parity): $325.9 billion (2012 est.)
    - GDP - real growth rate: 5% (2012 est.)
    - GDP - per capita (PPP): $3,600 (2012 est.)
- **Geographic characteristics:**
    - Size: 331,210 sq. km
    - Climate: tropical in south; monsoonal in north with hot, rainy season (May to September) and warm, dry season (October to March)
- **Political risk:** Although public support for the government has waned, and disputes over land tenure and freedom of speech will fuel popular discontent, there is no prospect of major internal instability. The government will continue to crack down on bloggers, pro-democracy activists and other critics.
- **Economic structure risk:** The government is planning a thorough overhaul of the country's inefficient and heavily indebted state-owned enterprises, but the process will be difficult and politically fraught, and progress will be slow.

Thailand

- **Demographic characteristics:**
    - Population size: 67,448,120 (July 2013 est.)
    - Population growth rate: 0.52% (2013 est.)
    - Urban population: 34.1% of total population (2011)
- **Economic Factors**
    - GDP (purchasing power parity): $662.6 billion (2012 est.)
    - GDP - real growth rate: 6.4% (2012 est.)
    - GDP - per capita (PPP): $10,300 (2012 est.)
- **Geographic characteristics:**
    - Size: 513,120 sq. km
    - Climate: tropical; rainy, warm, cloudy southwest monsoon (mid-May to September); dry, cool northeast monsoon (November to mid-March); southern isthmus always hot and humid
- **Political risk**: Yingluck Shinawatra has brought much-needed stability to Thailand's political scene since she became prime minister in 2011, but tensions persist. The military-backed establishment distrusts the populist character of her administration, and the future of her self-exiled brother, Thaksin Shinawatra, still has the potential to cause conflict.
- **Economic structure risk:** The Thai economy remains heavily dependent on exports, which account for about 60% of GDP. This makes it more vulnerable to global conditions than economies like the Philippines or Indonesia, where exports account for a smaller proportion of GDP.

Nigeria

- **Demographic characteristics:**
    - Population size: 174,507,539 (July 2013 est.)
    - Population growth rate: 2.54% (2013 est.)
    - urban population: 49.6% of total population

(2011)
- **Economic Factors**
    - GDP (purchasing power parity): $455.5 billion (2012 est.)
    - GDP - real growth rate: 6.3% (2012 est.)
    - GDP - per capita (PPP): $2,800 (2012 est.)
- **Geographic characteristics:**
    - Size: 923,768 sq. km
    - Climate: varies; equatorial in south, tropical in center, arid in north
- **Political risk:** Political risk will remain high. Islamist extremists threaten both regional and domestic stability. Meanwhile, splits in the ruling party along geographic and religious lines increase the risk of political violence.
- **Economic structure risk:** Despite robust growth in the non-oil sector, Nigeria's dependence on oil continues to leave it vulnerable to commodity price volatility. The US, historically a major purchaser of Nigerian oil, is reducing its imports as its domestic production of shale oil increases, which means there is a pressing need to expand Nigeria's Asian customer base.

Egypt

- **Demographic characteristics:**
    - Population size: 85,294,388 (July 2013 est.)
    - Population growth rate 1.88% (2013 est.)
    - Urban population: 43.5% of total population (2011)
- **Economic Factors**
    - GDP (purchasing power parity): $548.8 billion (2012 est.)
    - GDP - real growth rate: 2.2% (2012 est.)
    - GDP - per capita (PPP): $6,700 (2012 est.)
- **Geographic characteristics:**

- Size: 1,001,450 sq. km
- Climate: desert; hot, dry summers with moderate winters

- **Political risk:** Political uncertainty is extremely high following the ousting of the president, Mohammed Morsi. The Muslim Brotherhood will continue to organize protests demanding Mr. Morsi's reinstatement, prompting occasional violent clashes with the security forces and almost certainly the radicalization of some of its members.
- **Economic structure risk:** Tourism revenue—the second-largest foreign-currency source after oil and gas—has slid in the wake of the recent violence. Economic growth remains slow and is expected to dip below 2% in fiscal year 2013/14 (July-June).

Peru

- **Demographic characteristics:**
  - Population size: 29,849,303 (July 2013 est.)
  - Population growth rate: 1% (2013 est.)
  - Urban population: 77% of total population (2010)
- **Economic Factors**
  - GDP (purchasing power parity): $332 billion (2012 est.)
  - GDP - real growth rate: 6.3% (2012 est.)
  - GDP - per capita (PPP): $10,900 (2012 est.)
- **Geographic characteristics:**
  - Size: 1,285,216 sq. km
  - Climate: varies from tropical in east to dry desert in west; temperate to frigid in Andes
- **Political risk:** The administration of the president, Ollanta Humala, in office since 2011, has remained committed to Peru's business-friendly policy framework. However, income inequalities will persist and

dissatisfaction with the government's performance will continue to foment social protests, particularly in rural areas.
- **Economic structure risk:** As a result of Peru's over-reliance on a narrow basket of raw materials exports, the economy and business confidence are vulnerable to fluctuations in global commodity prices.

Bangladesh

- **Demographic characteristics:**
    - Population size: 163,654,860 (July 2013 est.)
    - Population growth rate: 1.59% (2013 est.)
    - Urban population: 28.4% of total population (2011)
- **Economic Factors**
    - GDP (purchasing power parity): $311 billion (2012 est.)
    - GDP - real growth rate: 6.1% (2012 est.)
    - GDP - per capita (PPP): $2,100 (2012 est.)
- **Geographic characteristics:**
    - Size: 143,998 sq. km
    - Climate: tropical; mild winter (October to March); hot, humid summer (March to June); humid, warm rainy monsoon (June to October)
- **Political risk:** The next parliamentary election must be held by January 24th 2014. Although the Awami League government is expected to complete its term, there is a risk of political turmoil if the opposition Bangladesh Nationalist Party carries out its threat to boycott the poll, as this would cast doubt on the validity of its outcome.
- **Economic structure risk:** Bangladesh's weak infrastructure and excessive reliance on textile exports pull down its rating for economic structure risk.

Pakistan

- **Demographic characteristics:**
    - Population size: 193,238,868 (July 2013 est.)
    - Population growth rate: 1.52% (2013 est.)
    - Urban population: 36.2% of total population (2011)
- **Economic Factors**
    - GDP (purchasing power parity): $523.9 billion (2012 est.)
    - GDP - real growth rate: 3.7% (2012 est.)
    - GDP - per capita (PPP): $2,900 (2012 est.)
- **Geographic characteristics:**
    - Size: 796,095 sq. km
    - Climate: mostly hot, dry desert; temperate in northwest; arctic in north
- **Political risk:** The sweeping mandate secured by the Pakistan Muslim League (Nawaz) in the May 2013 election will help to improve political stability, as will the selection of moderates to take over the key roles of army chief and head of the judiciary. However, the poor domestic security situation and jostling for power among the civilian executive mean that political risk will remain elevated.
- **Economic structure risk:** The domestic economy faces key structural threats. Its heavy reliance on imported oil leaves it vulnerable to volatility in global petroleum prices, while the agricultural sector depends on the monsoon.

Analysis of the initial screening:

Indonesia is clearly the most attractive market of the initial screening process: with a population over 250,000,000 million people a GDP of $1.237 trillion. Furthermore the countries surface is very large and Vibram shoes can be used very well in this terrain.

Egypt, Nigeria and Pakistan have a very high political risk at the moment. Therefore these countries are eliminated after the Initial screening.

Bangladesh has the lowest GDP and GDP per capita of the selected countries. Also there is a risk for political instability and the infrastructure is not very good. So this country has also been excluded from the second screening.

Thailand did not reach any of the highest values; nevertheless, the country seems also very attractive. It has a high GDP and GDP per capita.

The GDP of Vietnam is not very high; however there is a political stability and the government tries to improve the economic structure.

Peru has a very attractive GDP growth rate and high GDP per capita. Also the government seems very business friendly and the economic structure is ideal, also because of the high urbanization. However there is some political risk, but this country is selected for the second screening. Generally in all selected countries the climate is ideal to use Vibram five fingers for running outside. The winters are very moderate and the temperatures are high in most countries through the whole year.

Second Screening

Classification of countries after the initial screening:
1. Indonesia
2. Thailand
3. Peru
4. Vietnam

In the second screening, the attractiveness at micro level is measured. Specific indicators of the market that influence the distribution and sales of Vibram five fingers are analyzed:
- The size of the market for imported sports footwear
- Number of internet users: Because Vibram is promoting its product a lot through the internet

- Regulations: If there are any specific regulations that would influence the trade of Vibram five fingers in that country

(Data from United Nations Commodity Trade Statistics Database: http://comtrade.un.org/, www.indexmundi.com
www.internetworldstats.com
The Economist Intelligence Unit: www.eiu.com)

Indonesia

- **Market size**
    - Trade value of imports of sports footwear in 2009: $6,547,006
    - Trade value of imports of sports footwear in 2010: $5,912,755
    - Trade value of imports of sports footwear in 2011: $7,546,634
- **Internet users:** 55,000,000 (2012 est.)
- **Regulations that would influence Vibram:**
    - Ministry of Trade Regulation 68/2012 of October 2012 limits the number of outlets or branches that can be owned by a single retail company to 150. If it wants to have more outlets, then at least 40% of the total number of stores must be franchised locally. At least 80% of the goods to be sold in each franchise store must be obtained from local sources.
    - Regulation 27/2012, issued by the Ministry of Trade in May 2012, and its amendment, Regulation 59/2012 issued in October 2012, severely restrict imports. For example, producers previously licensed to import raw materials for their own use now may import "certain industrial goods" only for market testing and only if these goods are complementary to their products.

Thailand

- **Thailand Product usage:**
    - Trade value of imports of sports footwear in 2009: $5,486,086
    - Trade value of imports of sports footwear in 2010: $5,062,035
    - Trade value of imports of sports footwear in 2011: $6,991,083
- **Internet users**: 20,100,000 (2012 est.)
- **Regulations that would influence Vibram**:
    - The National Statistical Office (NSO) estimates that the number of unemployed workers stood at just 0.6% of the labor force at the end of the third quarter of 2012, down from 0.7% a year earlier. Minimum-wage hikes took effect April 1st 2012, and additional hikes are to be implemented from January 1st 2013; civil servants received a raise from April 1st 2013.
    - The government cut the corporate income tax rate to 23% (from 30%) in 2012, and plans to reduce this rate further, to 20%, in 2013. The cuts were announced to help companies compensate for hikes in the minimum wage and to make the country more competitive as a destination for foreign investments.

Peru

- **Product usage:**
    - Trade value of imports of sports footwear in 2009: $4,695,865
    - Trade value of imports of sports footwear in 2010: $3,984,640
    - Trade value of imports of sports footwear in 2011: $5,388,514

- **Internet users**: 10,785,573 (2012 est.)
- **Regulations that would influence Vibram**:
    - Peru is a founding member of the Pacific Alliance (Alianza del Pacífico) together with Chile, Colombia and Mexico—all of which already have bilateral free-trade agreements in place. Peru's Congress published Legislative Resolution 30053 (June 28th 2013) formally ratifying the agreement. The treaty expanded to include six observer nations in 2012 and seven in May 2013.
    - The administration published the National Workplace Safety and Health Policy (Supreme Decree 002-2013-TR, May 2nd 2013). The decree lays out six policy actions required to guarantee workplace safety, including a unified system for reporting workplace accidents and job-related illnesses, and progressive application of mandatory insurance for workers, among others.

Vietnam

- **Market size**
    - Trade value of imports of sports footwear in 2009: $1,326,593
    - Trade value of imports of sports footwear in 2010: $1,798,590
    - Trade value of imports of sports footwear in 2011: no data available
- **Internet users**: 31,034,900 (2012 est.)
- **Regulations that would influence Vibram**:
    - In June 2012, Vietnam's National Assembly passed a new Labor Code replacing a 1994 law and its amendments. The new law, effective from May 1st 2013, for the first time includes provisions on outsourcing, collective agree-

ments at the sectoral or industrial level and household helpers.
- As an economic-stimulus measure, the National Assembly in June 2012 reduced the corporate income tax (CIT) for 2012 by 30% for small and medium-sized enterprises (SMEs), with some exceptions. In another economic-stimulus measure, the government also issued Resolution No. 02/NQ-CP in January 2013 deferring for 3–6 months quarterly CIT and value-added tax payments by SMEs and labour-intensive enterprises, as well as companies engaged in the sale and leasing of houses.

Decision which country to enter

Indonesia and Thailand are the most attractive countries after the second screening. Indonesia has the highest trade value of imports of sport shoes in 2009, 2010 and 2011. Thailand has the highest growth rate comparing the imports of 2010 and 2011.

Indonesia has some strict limitations that would influence the import of Vibram Five Fingers. The Initial screening showed that the government has, at the moment, no intention to change these regulations. Thailand has the better regulations to trade in the country; however, there is a political risk.

Peru seems also interesting, but has a low number of internet users and trade value of imported sport shoes in 2011 is significally lower than in Indonesia and Thailand.

After the second screening, entering in the Vietnamese market doesn't seem interesting at all, because of the small market size.

For this project we decided to define a market entry strategy for Indonesia, because of the great advantage in the first and second screening.

SECTION 7: MARKET ENTRY STRATEGY FOR VIBRAM FIVE FINGERS

In most countries, we suppose, Vibram chose Licensing as an entry mode, because they have just one authorized distributor in most cases. Often this distributor also has an Internet site of "Vibram Five Fingers" in the language of the country, for example in Germany: www.vibram-fivefingers.de

In the USA and China Vibram made a foreign direct investment. The subsidiary in China is a big advantage for entering into Indonesia, because transportation of goods is quick and inexpensive.

Internet Marketing

Vibram uses Internet Marketing a lot to promote their product Vibram Five Fingers. On the website www.viramfivefingers.com the product and accessories are explained in detail. It's also possible to order them in an online store. With a tutorial called "Minimalist education" the company explains how to use their product in sports correctly. In the section "What's your story?" different persons are presented and they explain in Videos how and for what they are using Vibram Five Fingers.
Furthermore, Vibram has a Facebook page and a YouTube Channel. A suggestion to improve the official page and online store would be to make it available in more languages. At the moment it is just in English, Italian and Chinese. Vibram could cooperate

here with his partners and distributors to improve it.

Based on Communication Ministry data, at end of June 2011, there are 45 million Internet users in Indonesia, which 64 percent or 28 million users on the age of 15 to 19.
According to a survey by Nielsen's Southeast Asia Digital Consumer Report 48 percent of Internet users in Indonesia are using a mobile phone to access the Internet, whereas another 13 percent are using other handheld multimedia devices, the highest dependence on mobile Internet access in Southeast Asia. That shows that it would be very important to focus on mobile marketing also by developing new interesting apps for mobile devices.
Based on TNS research, Indonesia is the world's second largest number of Facebook users and the third largest number of Twitter users. It is also interesting that on Facebook an unofficial site of Vibram Five Fingers for Indonesia exists (https://www.facebook.com/vibramfivefingersindonesia). There a lot of Indonesians are discussing about the product and sharing their experience. This proofs that there is a great interest in using the product and Vibram should enter the market.

Entry strategy

Now Vibram has not entered the market and has not, according to the website, any authorized distributors in Indonesia. However some small local shops are selling their products. It's possible that the goods are imported from other Asian countries, like for example China or they are selling plagiats.
Indonesia would be an interesting market for Vibram, because it is emerging and outdoor activities are very popular there.
The Indonesian market is highly competitive. Markets with price wars are common and brands are very important. Consumer's income and the market for foreign brands are rising. In addition, costs should not be too high, because in the market are a lot of mid- and low income earners. To reach this audience a company

has to find the right channels.
It is difficult to get specialized, talented employees. Also for a company it is very important to consider the local culture, language and knowledge.
Marketing media are also different from elsewhere, for example, Unilever still utilizes door-to-door promotions in Indonesia.

According to the document: "Emerging Market Entry Candidates—Emerging Market Entry Candidates—Indonesia" from Accenture there are 3 principle entry modes for the Indonesian market:

Go it alone: Building a local presence from the ground. Companies should focus on the island of Java. There the best infrastructure exists and low industry regulation and FDI requirements are necessary. The local customers recognize strong brand equity. Also hiring people is easier there than in other regions.
For example, the shoe company Bata established its own distribution channel and training for distributors in Java. Their value preposition is to sell high quality shoes at an affordable price. Bata is able to develop local talent through marketing and education campaigns.

Partner: By cooperation with a partner it can be easier to gain access to local expertise. It is easier to deal with market entry restrictions or regulations. Furthermore the brand image of a partner can be used to immediately gain access to qualified and skilled staff.

Acquire: This strategy is ideal for firms which want to enter with fast in a highly regulated market and want to penetrate an already competitive market. Also industry knowledge and existing infrastructure, customers, talent and networks can be gained.

From our perspective the right entry mode would be to cooperate with a partner at the beginning. The reasons for this are the strict regulations in Indonesia. Also by doing that, Vibram will get to know the local market and the differences to other markets. They should try to find a distributor, which they can license

like in other countries. If it's not possible to find a distributor or a partner, Vibram should try to go for it alone. But before doing that a detailed analysis of the Indonesian market is required.
Because of the high amount of Internet users we definitely recommend to create an online store for Indonesia. In addition, viral marketing through Social Networks should be easy to achieve, because of the large user base and interest in Vibram Five Fingers.

Operating model considerations:

It's very important to choose the right operating model. These elements have to be taken into consideration in order to create an environment that integrates people, information and technology:

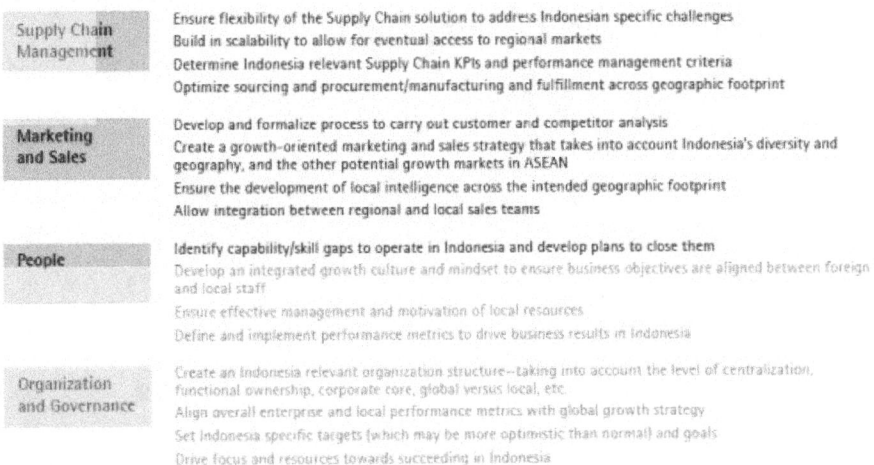

Supply Chain Management: Here it would be possible to integrate the subsidiary in China into the Supply Chain. Therefore, Vibram can ensure flexibility and scalability. The fulfillment (Transportation of the good to the customer) is a bit complicated in Indonesia, because the country is divided into many islands. It's not easy to predict the time of the shipping of an order.

Marketing and sales: Here of course Vibram has to consider its competitors. However the product (Vibram Five Fingers) is unique and the company holds a patent for it. So Vibram has no direct competitors in this field, but many indirect competitors which sell sports footwear. Furthermore it is very imported to understand the cultural specifics in Indonesia

People: In this area one of the crucial factors is hire the right people. That isn't easy in Indonesia. If a company wants to be successful in Indonesia it has to consider its local resources. Some regulations by the government also require this.

Organization and Governance: From our point of view, Vibram has a polycentric orientation, because it uses a differentiated approach from market to market. We think that Vibram uses a friendly persuasion to coordinate its subsidiaries. Maybe for the market entry in Indonesia Vibram could use the approach of a transnational firm by making the subsidiary in China the executor and strategic leader for this project.

APPENDIX 1: EVOLUTION OF THE INDICES

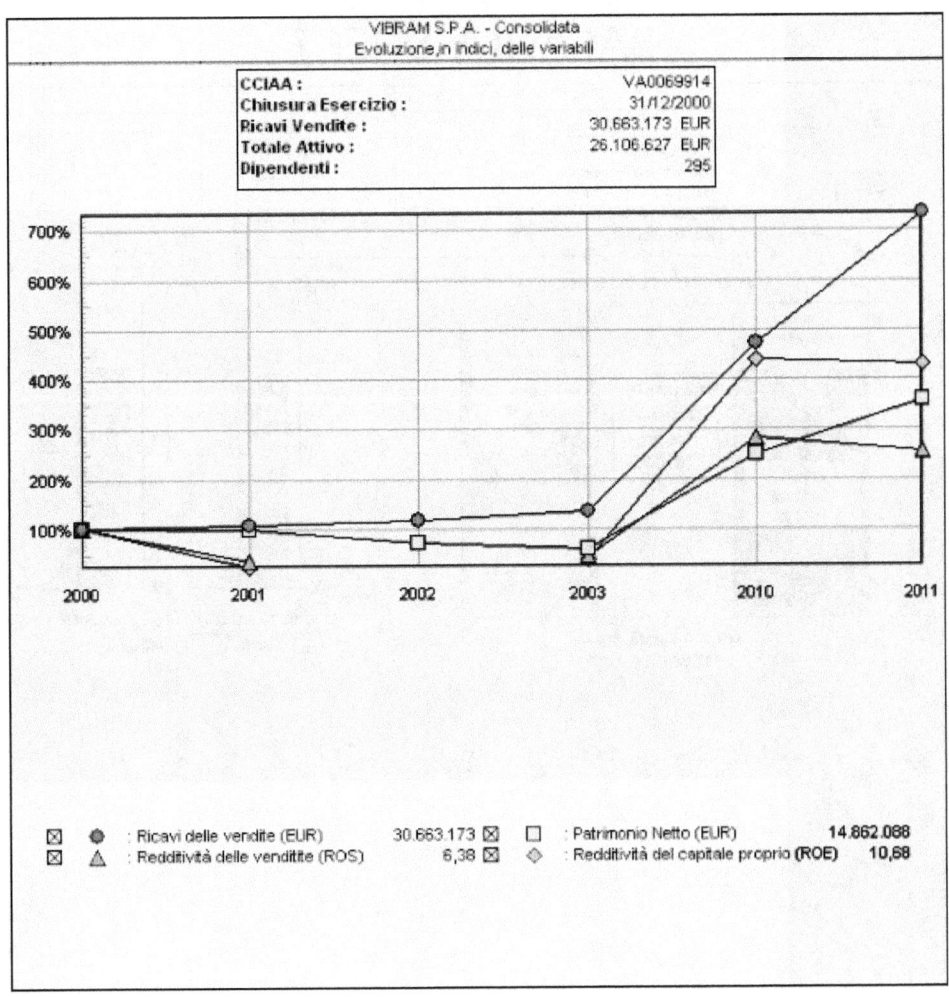

APPENDIX 2: GRAPHIC ILLUSTRATION OF THE BALANCE SHEET

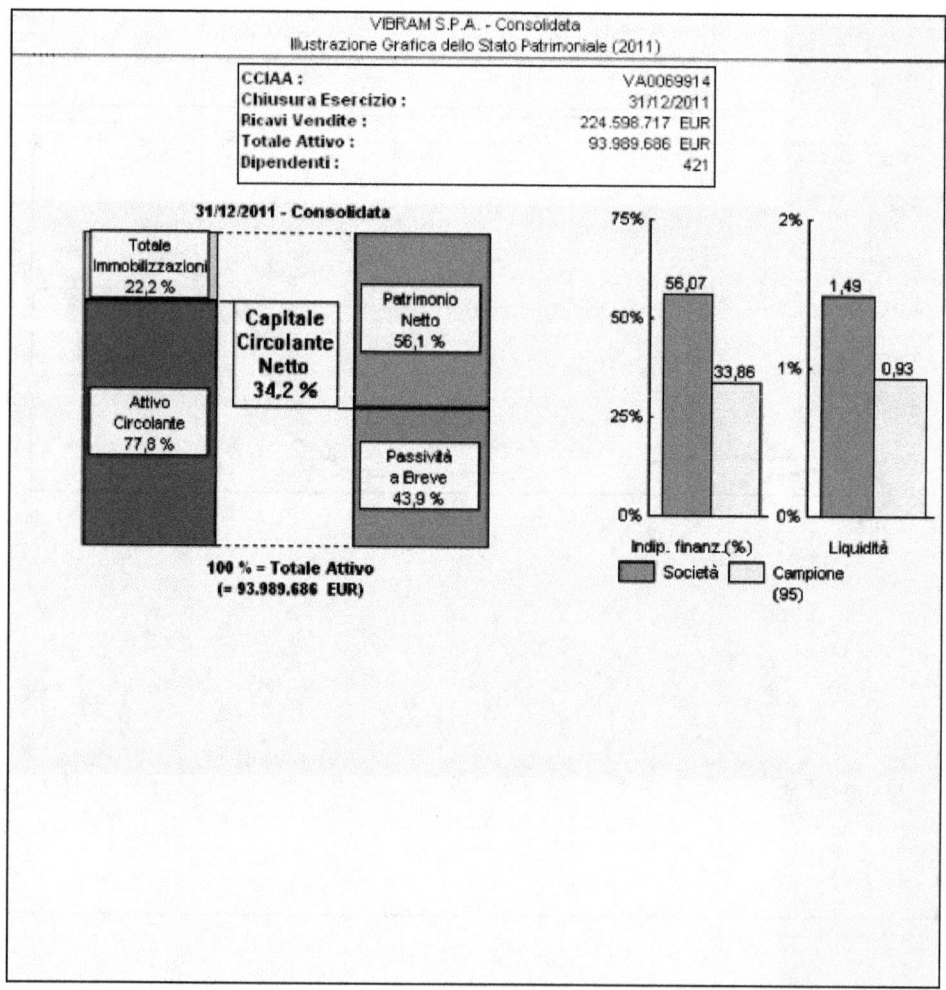

APPENDIX 3: GRAPHIC ILLUSTRATION OF THE COMPANY'S PROFITS

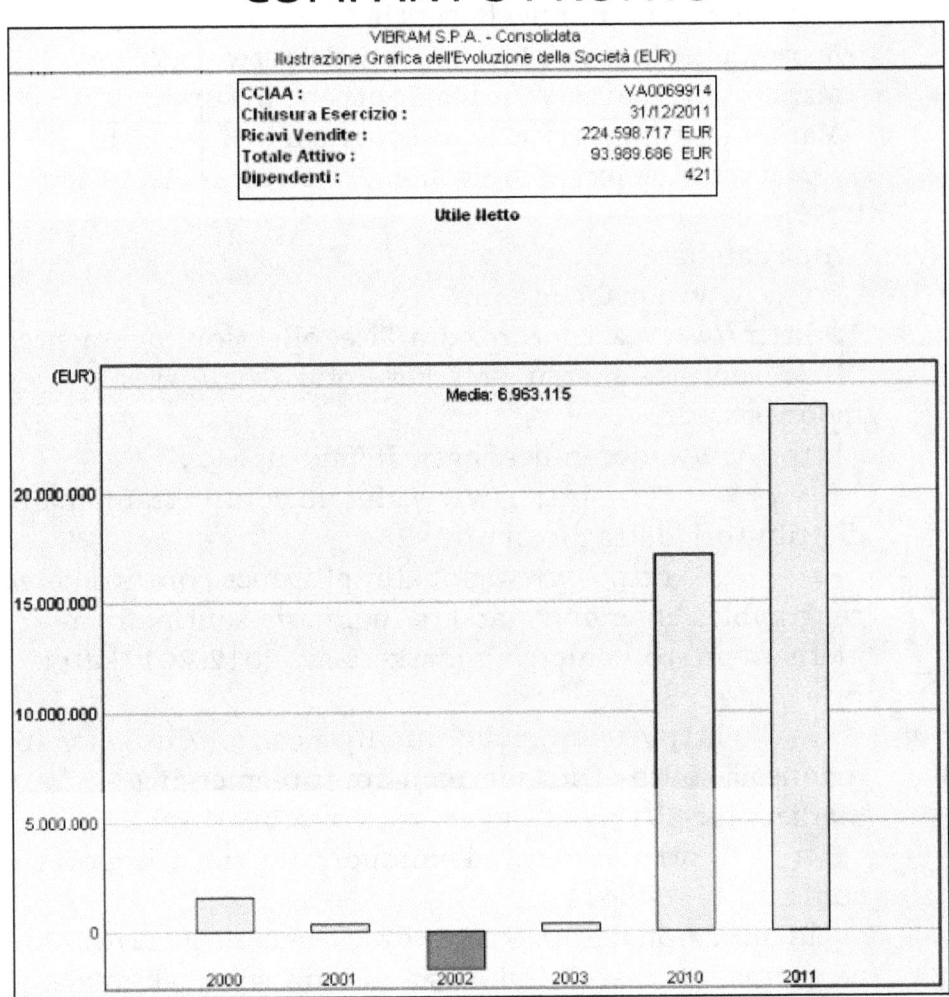

BIBLIOGRAPHY:

- Slides from Prof. Carolina Guerini and Prof. Željko Šuman
- http://www.vibramfivefingers.it/storia.aspx
- http://www.vibramfivefingers.it
- Market Line Industry Profile, Global Footwear, 2013
- Market Line Industry Profile, Footwear in Europe, 2013
- Market Line Industry Profile, Footwear in Italy, 2013
- Market Line Industry Profile, Footwear in Asia-Pacific, 2013
- Aida database
- http://www.quabaug.com/
- http://www.accenture.com/SiteCollectionDocuments/PDF/Accenture-Emerging-Market-Entry-Candidates-Indonesia.pdf
- http://www.vibramfivefingers.it/find_us.aspx
- http://www.vibram.com/vibramrepair/distributori_dettaglio.php?id=28
- http://www.globalintelligence.com/insights/geographies/emerging-markets/indonesia-south-africa-vietnam-are-top-emerging-markets-for-2012-2017-after-bric
- http://www.globalintelligence.com/insights/all/indonesia-south-africa-vietnam-are-top-emerging-markets-for-2012-2017-after-bric#ixzz2mY4GnhXR
- http://www.indexmundi.com/trade/imports/?commodity=640411
- http://smpn2parungkuda.wordpress.com/2011/07/28/pengguna-internet-di-indonesia-didominasi-anak-muda/
- http://www.thejakartapost.com/news/2011/07/12/ri-highly-dependent-mobile-internet.html
- http://www.thejakartapost.com/news/2011/05/31/

cheap-smartphones-change-ri-internet-behavior-survey.html
- United Nations Commodity Trade Statistics Database: http://comtrade.un.org/

---

[1] http://www.quabaug.com/
[2] Data extracted from Market Line databases

www.ingramcontent.com/pod-product-compliance
Lightning Source LLC
Chambersburg PA
CBHW050313220526
45465CB00005B/1967